CW00542009

MOTHER TONGUE

Rose Ausländer

MOTHER

TONGUE

Translated by Jean Boase-Beier
and Anthony Vivis

1995

Published by Arc Publications
Nanholme Mill, Shaw Wood Road
Todmorden, Lancs. OL14 6DA

Translation copyright © 1995
          Jean Boase-Beier / Anthony Vivis
Introduction copyright © 1995
          Jean Boase-Beier / Anthony Vivis
Production copyright © 1995 Arc Publications

Design by Tony Ward
Printed at Arc & Throstle Press
Nanholme Mill, Shaw Wood Road
Todmorden, Lancs. OL14 6DA

ISBN 0 946407 77 0

Acknowledgements
The poems on pages 32, 39, 61, 73 and 83 are
published in German by Pfaffenweiler Presse
(copyright 1980), the remainder are published by
S. Fischer Verlag.

The Publishers acknowledge financial assistance
from Yorkshire and Humberside Arts and the
Arts Council of England

**Arc Publications International Poets
Series Editor: Michael Hulse**

TRANSLATORS' NOTE

Rose Ausländer's poems, especially the later ones, to which most of those collected here belong, are written in a direct style, in an outwardly simple form. Yet the simplicity is often deceptive. While the experiences she shares with us – of love, isolation, friendship, struggle, death – have a surface value we can all recognise, both style and content go far beyond the everyday. Behind the vividness of her imagery and the calm, often conversational tone in which she addresses us, lie philosophical profundity, intense passion, and scarcely bearable suffering. Smoke, ashes, dust, hunger, crystal soon to be shattered – these are some of the disturbing images which occur and recur in her poems.

Thus, while we never leave the real world when reading Rose Ausländer, we never feel far from the magical and sinister realms of the imagination. Sometimes her poems lead us back into historical, mythical and classical worlds. At other times they open up insights which confront us with a new view of the immediate present.

In their subtlety and their strength these poems offer many opportunities to explore language and form. It has been a great joy to recreate them in the English language.

Jean Boase-Beier / Anthony Vivis

CONTENTS

Introduction · 8

Part One

Dust that Joins · 15 · Einheitsstaub
Mother Tongue · 16 · Muttersprache
Words · 17 · Sprache
The Net · 18 · Das Netz
The Architects · 19 · Die Architekten
As If · 20 · Als Gäbe Es
Always the Word · 21 · Immer Das Wort
Sentences · 22 · Sätze
Beyond · 23 · Jenseits
I am Holding Fast · 24 · Ich Halte Mich Fest
Castles in the Air · 25 · Luftschlösser

Part Two

Paul Celan · 29 · Paul Celan
Georg Trakl · 30 · Georg Trakl
Rainbow I · 31 · Regenbogen I
Mystery · 32 · Menschlich II
Experience · 33 · Erfahrung
Idyll · 34 · Idylle
Games · 35 · Menschlich
Awaiting Transformation · 36 · Erwartung Und Verwandlung
Essential Mother · 37 · Letzte Mutter
Whilst I am Drawing Breath · 38 · Während Ich Atem Hole
Snow · 39 · Schnee
Faith · 40 · Bekenntnis

Part Three

July · 43 · Juli
The Unheard Heart · 44 · Das Unhörbare Herz
The Spell of the Cuckoo · 45 · Der Kuckuck Zaubert
Times Table · 46 · Das Einmaleins
Hunger · 47 · Hunger
Chamomile · 48 · Kamillen
No Other Way · 50 · Nichts Übrig
Atlantis Always Glittering · 51 · Immer Atlantis

Part Four

Your House · 55 · Dein Haus
The Carnival Over · 56 · Nach Dem Karneval
Mills Made of Wind · 57 · Mühlen Aus Wind
In a Sieve · 58 · Mit Dem Sieb
In Those Years · 59 · In Jenen Jahren
Smoke · 60 · Rauch
And Sometimes the Wind · 61 · Und Manchmal Der Wind
And Shut Out Their Love · 62 · Damit Kein Licht Uns Liebe
Strident Silence · 63 · Schallendes Schweigen
Willow Word · 64 · Weidenwort
A Day in Exile · 65 · Ein Tag im Exil
Ark · 66 · Arche
Ashes · 67 · Asche
When April Comes · 68 · Der Nächste April

Part Five

On the Wing · 71 · Im Flug
Beneath My Skin · 72 · Hinter Der Haut
In You · 73 · In Dir
Love III · 74 · Liebe III
Love · 75 · Liebe
The Island · 76 · Die Insel

Part Six

Old Grey-Haired Woman · 79 · Alte Ergraute Frau
Coffins · 81 · Särge
Signs · 82 · Spannung
When I Have Gone · 83 · Wenn Ich Vergehe
Exchange · 84 · Austausch
Night · 85 · Nacht

Part Seven

Still the Night · 89 · Stille Nacht
Questions · 90 · Mit Fragen
On the Barricades · 91 · Auf Barrikaden

INTRODUCTION

Rose Ausländer was born in 1901 in the city of Chernovtsy in the Carpathian foothills, in what was then part of Austria-Hungary, to German-speaking Jewish parents. She was to lead a very unsettled life, fleeing occupation and persecution, living alternately in America and in Europe, writing partly in German and partly in English. There were, however, elements of stability in this uneasy life. One was poetry itself and the writing of poetry. So it is not surprising that a constant theme of her poems is words, and the power of words. She celebrates those "who are skilled with words", who are free to believe in their value and their healing power, in the power of the imagination, those "who fly to the stars".

Her childhood in Chernovtsy, a town with a full and rich cultural life, was very happy, if perhaps somewhat over-protected. The initial upheaval came during the First World War, when the family was forced to flee, first to Vienna and later to Budapest, to escape the Romanian occupation. Many of her poems reflect the happiness and the mysteries of childhood; she writes, though, not only of fairies and nymphs, but also of dragons. The poems express joy and security: "sleep yourself awake / my child / I will light your way", but often in the same breath there is fear and misery, the pain of "the children who played in the fire". Typically, in *Snow*, the childhood figures of Snow White and the Seven Dwarves appear, but in the background "beyond the mountains" there is the threatening presence of the "dark queen", who follows Snow White as inevitably as night comes after day.

After the war, Chernovtsy became part of Romania, and the family returned. Rose studied Philosophy and Literature at Chernovtsy University and became familiar not only with the literature of Goethe, Hölderlin, Trakl and Kafka, but also with the philosophy of Plato and Spinoza, and of Constantin Brunner, with whom she was to exchange many letters.

In 1921, after her father's death had brought financial hardship upon the family, Rose and her friend Ignaz Ausländer emigrated to America. They married in 1923 in New York. It was at this time that her first poems were published in anthologies. After seven years of marriage, the couple divorced, and Rose Ausländer returned to Chernovtsy, as she was to do many times during her life. Her poems were published there in a number of anthologies and literary journals. A first collection, *Der Regenbogen* (*The Rainbow*), appeared in 1939, receiving good reviews. But it was not particularly successful. As a Jewish writer, Rose Ausländer was treated with contempt in Germany. She again went to live in the USA because of the vulnerable situation of the Jews in Eastern Europe, but her mother's illness prompted her to return almost immediately. She took work in a factory, continuing to write poetry throughout this time, and in fact, as many writers in similar circumstances have found, her writing provided her with a sense of stability and perhaps of transcendence. In 1941, when Chernovtsy was occupied by the Nazis, she and her family were sent to live in the Jewish ghetto. For more than a year, she and her mother were forced to hide, moving from cellar to cellar, helped by courageous friends. She continued to write poetry. And at this time she first met Paul Antschel, who was later to call himself Paul Celan.

The hardships of a life in hiding, the constant fear of Nazi terror, the horror of the concentration camps are all present in her many poems which speak, often indirectly, of those years. These poems are filled with images of hunger and poverty, of wounds, blood, coffins, fire and ashes, smoke.

Other poems speak, again indirectly, of the mother for whose sake she endured these hardships. In later poems, the mother becomes a symbol for the air we are destroying, the "essential mother", or for the healing power of language: "mother tongue, you piece me together".

The ghetto in Chernovtsy was liberated by the Russians in 1944, but life was not easy for the German-speaking Jews, many of whom were now subjected to terrible persecution by their "liberators". Rose Ausländer was comparatively lucky, finding work in a library, and managing to make contact with many writers as part of a literary circle. In 1946, the Northern part of Bukovina, including Chernovtsy, became part of the Ukraine. That year, she left for New York. Her health was very poor, and she suffered a complete breakdown when her mother, for whom she had been trying to obtain a visa to join her in New York, died in 1947.

For the next few years, as she tried to come to terms with her mother's death, she rejected her mother tongue, writing no more in German but publishing many poems and translations in English. It was not until ten years after her mother's death that, having visited Europe in the meantime and revived her friendship with Paul Celan, she started to write in German again, changing her poetic style quite radically. Partly as a result of the influence of Celan's work, she abandoned the strict rhyme schemes and metrical patterns of her earlier work for a freer but more compressed style. It is to these later poems, written after a long silence in her mother tongue, that most of those collected here belong. Full rhyme has now frequently given way to less obvious assonance and alliteration, and strict metre to the rhythms of colloquial speech. As in her earlier poems, there is a complete absence of punctuation, giving scope for multiple interpretation. It is this later style which has come, in German-speaking countries, to be most closely associated with the work of Rose Ausländer. An example is MÜHLEN AUS WIND:

9

Das tägliche Brot
kommt uns teuer zu stehen

Mühlen aus Wind
mahlen Sandmehl

Am Rand einer Rinde
ernährt sich
die Not

Gib was du nicht hast
Liebe dem Nachbarn

Was suchst du
im flüchtenden Wasser
Narziß

There is a tight, though unobtrusive, structure of syntactic patterning in this poem. The repetition of the etymologically related *Mühlen, mahlen, –mehl* gives iconic force to the description of a mill turning. The slant-rhyme of *Rand – Rinde*, the full rhyme of *Brot – Not* underline this repetitive structure which represents not just the actual turning of a mill but an associated lack of progression which itself echoes the negative circular hollowness of mills which are not driven by wind but are actually made of it, of famine which feeds where people do not, of non-existent love, of only oneself mirrored in the water.

A poem like this seems simple, almost cosy at first glance. But the comforting images of daily bread, mills, flour, water are used as vehicles to speak of famine, deprivation, lack of love, self-obsession. It is this juxtaposition of the everyday, the colloquial, with an unexpected subtle menace which gives the poems their power to unsettle. It is also this very juxtaposition which renders the translator's task so difficult. The lexis must be kept simple; these are threats inherent in everyday life. It is difficult, though, to re-create a repetition like *Mühlen, mahlen, –mehl* in a language which renders them as non-alliterating *mills, grind, flour*.

Here is our version:

MILLS MADE OF WIND

Our daily bread
comes at great cost

Mills made of wind

10

grind the grains of sand

Famine feeds
on the edge of a crust

Give your neighbour the love
you have never had

What is it you are seeking
in the fleeting water
Narcissus

Here *mills* have been made to alliterate with *made, grind* with *grains*, and half-rhyme has been added in *wind, grind,* and *sand* to preserve at least some of the circular monotony. The alliteration of *Am Rand einer Rinde* has been echoed in *famine feeds,* and the rhyme of *Brot* and *Not,* which in the German serves to emphasise their contrasting nature, is at least partially captured in *cost* and *crust,* slant rhymes which also fall on contrasting concepts.

In many of her later poems Ausländer uses this combination of repetitive phonetic (and often also syntactic) patterning with simple vocabulary and contrasting concepts. She also develops the use of key words which run like a thread through all her later work: dream, breath, gold, white, crystal, stars, ashes.

In 1965 Rose Ausländer returned for the final time to Europe, living in Düsseldorf and travelling a great deal. Her second collection of poetry, *Blinder Sommer* (*Blind Summer*), appeared that year. Though it received one or two excellent reviews, it did not reach a large audience. Greater fame came with her third collection, *36 Gerechte* (*36 of The Just*), published in 1967. Her work began to be widely anthologised and she received a number of literary prizes.

After this, many collections of her poetry appeared, bringing her both critical acclaim and widespread fame, especially in Germany. By 1981 her health had became very frail, and she wrote her last poem. Perhaps she had enough faith "in poetry weaving humanity's myth" to know the answer to the question she had asked in *When I Have Gone:*

When I go away
from our forgetful earth
will you speak my words
a while for me?

She died in 1988.

J.B-B. / A.V.

11

ONE

DUST THAT JOINS

We who are weavers of words

heretics who believe
we fly to the stars
in love with the earth
which we burn to ashes
on funeral pyres

and we sing hymns
to the electric dust

dust that joins us together
building up
breaking down

MOTHER TONGUE

I have changed
from myself into myself
from moment to moment

sprung into fragments
on the word path

Mother tongue
you piece me together

a human mosaic

WORDS

Keep me in your service
my whole life long
let me breathe in you

I thirst for you
drink you word for word
my source

Your angry glitter
winter-word

Lilac-fine
you bloom in me
word of spring

I follow you
even into sleep
spell out all your dreams

We speak the same language
we love each other

THE NET

I want to say something
one word
which says it all

not
I am who I am
not regale me with
gemstones coins countries

The word fails me
and I fall silent

fall into a net
with syllable meshes
woven of time

THE ARCHITECTS

A house built of imagination
roof of thoughts

Not
words of syllable foam

Spring courts you
with many colours
this Summer's artery
beats in your ear
for you Autumn bleeds
inventor of Winter
your vision is so white

Yes they are still there
builders of immaterial dwellings
behind the concrete and stone
they create a room
for us all

AS IF

As if there were
heaven
and earth
looking up

As if there were
dull brown
and radiant blue

As if there were
heaven-words
and words of earth

As if there were
your words
my words
you or me

ALWAYS THE WORD

When I say gold
I mean the word

When I say word
I mean
gold new world people

you and me talking

SENTENCES

Crystals
uneven in form
compact transparent
everything behind them
visible

This obsessive search
for binding words
sentence after sentence
to reach even further
into this known
unknowable world

BEYOND

We shall find
each other again

you will write
an ending
for words begun

sayings for those
who hear
beyond all bounds

I AM HOLDING FAST

Who has torn
the rainbow
from my field of vision

I tried to tie it fast
to seven words

My eyes are drowning
in the rain

I am holding fast
to the paper
this sheet of paper

CASTLES IN THE AIR

The swallows
have gone
out of the land of childhood

Gone is
the land of childhood

The children
all grown old

In no man's land
I build castles in the air
out of paper

TWO

PAUL CELAN

Sealed
in hermetic silence
his word
squeezed bleeding
from the capsule of the heart
borne
on wings black as stars
releases blinding light
by whose shadow
he is cruelly
illuminated

GEORG TRAKL

Melancholia
twilight-indigo

A whisper of dust

In the leafy shadows
beasts fall to their knees

This Autumn is a
golden carcass

Wood
seeping wound

*

Georg
Your wound
has never closed

RAINBOW I

An encounter
wide as the heavens
between water and sun

Seven colours
harnessed together
so that the bow
will not break

Can this team of seven
take away the seven deadly sins?

MYSTERY

Look for a while
into the clouds
and you will often see
ogres and angels

The leaves too
have many faces
Sometimes I recognise
a friend
within their tracery

At times how human
familiar things become

But human beings
are mysteries
I am trying to solve

EXPERIENCE

Gather experience
in woods mountains
cities

in the eyes
of men and women

in talk
in silence

IDYLL

In the hut
with moss-covered walls
in that isolated place
the names are hard to read

In the yard
a happy dog scratches
its sloping signature
into the earth
and turns turns turns
breathless
round the breath
of grasses

GAMES

In the window stands a landscape
six houses
each with its own small plot

Trees talk
the poplars say hello
without nodding their heads

Someone has taken them seriously
and given this lane
their name

Dead straight the paths
where arcs of water criss-cross
a grid of liquid crystal

Time and the seasons
breathing in and out

We are human
we enjoy these little games

AWAITING TRANSFORMATION

The days are growing thin
From the mesh of branches hang
pledges spoken by lovers
and left behind like nuts
from the hoard of a forgetful squirrel
White veils waft overhead
curtains at cobalt windows

Deep sounds come from the lake
where fear lies hidden
under the cheek of the water
You hear the muted murmur
of threat and transformation
Domesticated cliffs wait
patiently for metamorphosis
they smile and their silver teeth
close on the elements
blades of grass still keep their fragile shape

their own lives and the ties
with their own race, the turf

Shadows shake the park benches
winds sway the thinning leaves
children abandon their toys
to chase the sun
Then balloons appear
climbing eagerly
They seem to believe they are birds
the heavens their home
they celebrate their own ascent
aeroplanes with booming metal voices
rap out the anonymous words
of utility

Once again the lake echoes
with compressed twilight sounds
We shudder
in fear of the warnings from the water
and hold our breath
awaiting transformation

ESSENTIAL MOTHER

Born of blood and water
formed in the forest
of the city

One jungle
borders upon another
divided by the knife

Flying high as light
swimming in the flood of poison

Essential mother
air
we are destroying her

WHILST I AM DRAWING BREATH

Whilst I am drawing breath
the air has changed colour
leaves and grass have dried in different tones
a banner of straw hangs from the sky

Whilst I am drawing breath a figure
freezes to death in my nerves
I hear the silhouette of an
angel dying away

Now it is time
To shape a dream in shades of grey
it has grown uneasy and come to rest on my
head whilst I am drawing breath

Meanwhile the sun has glazed over and
sprung cracks. I look for its
flawless form in the Hudson but
in those greying eyes its
outlines are blurred
From the North there comes a
sudden hand which drives
the drops into the
Atlantic Ocean
whilst I am drawing breath

SNOW

Snow falls
the world turns white

In the sun
that white glitters
in every colour

White stars
blossom in the air

On the horizon
beyond the mountains
look: Snow White
and the Seven Dwarves

At night
the white is black
black as the dark queen
beyond the mountains

FAITH

I profess my faith

in the earth and its
dangerous mysteries

in rain in snow
in tree and mountain

in that murderous mother
the sun in water and
the water's flight

in milk in bread

in poetry
weaving humanity's myth

in humanity

I profess my faith
with all the words
that create me

THREE

JULY

In the arteries of thorns
the cleansed blood
is anointed by sun

Even the fingers of thistles
have delicate nails
in the lark-light

Stags hold
the heavens
in their antlers

When will you
emerge from the Garden
Adam
your span of immortality has ended

Your companion
swallows beneath her veil
throws the apple at your feet
earth

THE UNHEARD HEART

In the arteries of everyday
the earth fairy's unheard heart beats
its soundless drum

Beats in time with the musical clock of planetary pulses
the needles of seconds
cannot wound it
It is invulnerable
to time and all
assaults of contact

Sometimes when it is very still
very white all round me
very primeval within me
I hear the unheard heart
in my breathing
like a clock made of air
then the melody of the music-box
is alive in my temples
its tones muted like the moving spheres

THE SPELL OF THE CUCKOO

The cuckoo among the leaves
casts its ritual spell
in smooth two-syllable notes
Distinctly we hear
its magic mouth
calling the Summer

In foreign lands the weather fairy
keeps the snow prisoner
pools of sun grow
into lakes where willows bathe
and swallows

In the nest an egg comes to life
in Pan's arms
the nightingale wakens

A brief ballet of midges
draws bright circles
on the timeless page of the air

TIMES TABLE

The prisoners in the tower
have imprisoned their warder
and with him they recite
the times table of the hours

Labyrinths are embroidered
into the tapestry of the walls
passages leading nowhere
but to an Open Sesame

At night the prisoners
gather up the world in secret
bring it into the tower
divide it fairly
amongst themselves
In the morning every
trace is gone
the cells once again
gloomy rectangles
without birds or waterfalls

The prisoners share
secretive greetings
tinged with the faint glow of the world
and with their warder they recite
the times table of the hours

HUNGER

In my prison
I dream the apple

Lord grant me
my sins

(Out of your rib Eden
Adam out of mine)

Blindly peering
through the peep-hole
Secretively I plant
the word in this cell
exhorting the apple to grow

Out of the angel's
limited line of vision
the tree
tall as a dream

Apple-green cherry-red
deadly tree
of bitter nightshade

CHAMOMILE

Chamomile
The years of greening
peopled with fauns and fairies
run riot in my skull
And nymphs go on making their
forest mischief
in the machine room

Golden tea
A silk dress rustles in the corner
Angels hold up the mirror
A choir of children below the window
a symphony of frogs and crickets

Universe
chockful of corpses and catastrophes
labyrinthine lands
guarded by dragons
roses not knowing that
a shadow presses down on them
the rump of the robot

Let your mask fall
the soap-bubbles spray
from your lips on to
mint and poppy
the down of dandelions
floats over the lake
inside the cup of a water-lily
Undine whispers in a muted voice
like a mother on Friday
in front of the candles

Electric birds
in metal trees
screech you awake
the ring with its family crest of lime
rolls from your thumb
you put on your coat of steel
your hair in leaves of wire
picks up aerials
in your nostrils the scent
of chamomile subsides

NO OTHER WAY

Forgive me
sea
I can swim
neither at your surface
nor below
to discover unruly legends

There is no other way
but invention

ATLANTIS ALWAYS GLITTERING

Atlantis is always sinking
beyond our astounded gaze
it is always a breathing green
a poppied red
cypress and marble
there are always celebrations in swaying gardens
well-proportioned people
always holy and delicate and suffering alone

They well up in us
sink down in us
we are their tombs
And always in the rubble of palaces
their deaths are alive in us
with all the enchanted cypresses
serpents and Edens

We are always interwoven
with the radiance of resurrected
cities and empires
we can always feel the crystal of the earth
burning in our eyes
Atlantis is always glittering
beyond the shore-line of our hearts

FOUR

YOUR HOUSE

The sun says
sleep yourself awake
my child
I will light your way

The rain
I am weeping for the
children who played in the fire
weep with me
my child

Ash
choking on the words
my house is your house

THE CARNIVAL OVER

The carnival over, the lean times came
the days of mouldy bread and bitter herbs
I hungered for the flesh of figs
I thirsted for oranges

I joined a caravan and crossed
the desert on a date hunt
Sand stuck in my throat
The hump of a camel
became my home
The hours like ovens round my head
the constellations Scorpio and Crucifix

At daybreak the horizon grew red
with a mirage which would not come closer
Only one oasis gave us shelter
its water smelt of poppies moon and fire
its dates and figs had shrivelled up

MILLS MADE OF WIND

Our daily bread
comes at great cost

Mills made of wind
grind the grains of sand

Famine feeds
on the edge of a crust

Give your neighbour the love
you have never had

What is it you are seeking
in the fleeting water
Narcissus

IN A SIEVE

In a sieve
I scoop up water
to drive this mill

keeping the sails in motion
with my breath

grinding the meal
of hunger

IN THOSE YEARS

In those years
time was frozen:
ice as far as the soul could reach

From those roofs
hung daggers
The whole town made
of inflexible glass
people dragging
sacks of snow
to frozen funeral pyres

One day a song
of golden flakes
fell upon the snow-field:
        "Do you know the country
        where the lemon-trees flower?"
A country where lemons flower?
What land flowers now?
The snowmen
did not know.

The ice grew thicker
sent down
white roots
into the marrow of our years

SMOKE

This fractured column
smoke

    And the columns tremble like this
in the Greek temples
in the Athens of my dreams

From the eyes
of sated man-eaters
smoke surges
and in it my words
have blackened

I must swallow the bitter pill
of the smoke of thirty years
my voice chokes
in the smoke of the endless ghetto
in beautiful
barbaric lands

    Put out the flames brother
when no one is watching

AND SOMETIMES THE WIND

Fog golden eyes wailing voices

The dead glide hand in hand
through the fog
through watchful golden eyes
and pass
down alleys of wailing voices

Before things fell apart
there was a beautiful race
walking upright
perfectly proportioned
creatures who
ran with the stars
mastered the sun
Those days were sublime
when shells and tiny pebbles
had doors to eternity

Now it is all confusion
and the fog horn moans
in the ears of the dead

And sometimes a wind comes
with keen scissors
cutting the fog into strips
between them stretches of inflamed blue

Fog golden eyes wailing voices

and sometimes the wind

AND SHUT OUT THEIR LOVE

They came
with guns and jagged banners
shot down the moon and all the stars
and shut out their light
and shut out their love

That day we buried the sun
And there was eternal night

STRIDENT SILENCE

There were some who escaped

And hands crept
out of the night
brick-red with the blood of those
they had murdered

It was a strident spectacle
an image formed of flames
music made of fire.
Then death fell silent
Fell silent

This was a strident silence
Smiling stars glinted
among the twigs

Those who have escaped wait at the harbour
Where the wrecked ships lie at anchor
Almost like cradles
but without the mother and child

WILLOW WORD

I call out to the river
my willow word
bowed on the bank
from every root bleeding
and torn
the clods of soil
that held me fast

Nights
knotted together
into a single night
in an iron sleep
I drink
abstract stars
in the river
I call out
my willow word
to the sunken souls
the squall has
driven down
to the pebbles

A DAY IN EXILE

A day in exile
a house without doors or windows

Time drawn on a tablet
charcoal on white

In a chest
the mortal masks
Adam
Abraham
Ahasuerus
Who knows all the names

A day in exile
when the hours stoop
to climb out of the cellar
and into the room

Shadows gathered
round the oil-lamp's eternal flame
tell their stories
along the walls
with ten dark fingers

ARK

On the sea
an ark made of stars
is waiting

for the ashes
that survive
the flood of fire

ASHES

In the rain of ashes
is the trace of your name

It was
a perfect word

Fire
consumed it

I threw my cloak of dust
upon the flames

Behind that blind gaze
your eyes
draw me to you

WHEN APRIL COMES

To see you once again
when April comes
see you free of ashes –
can it really happen?

The sun an Empress
in her cloak of breath
free without fear
the lark so real

Not so long ago –
for history a mere intake of breath

But when in these days of dynamite
have we the right to write
on our beds of straw?

That ancient dream has stayed intact
within our bloodstream:
Eden, angel, you

Will this coming April
emerge unscathed?
Have I the right to see you once
again free of ashes
entangled in verses?

FIVE

ON THE WING

On the wing
you seek freedom

where words
have all been lost

you find language
which speaks of love

BENEATH MY SKIN

You
morning midday at night
a different person

I know you
from the movement in your eyes

You smile
you speak you promise

The words beneath your skin
have a different ring

Which cannot be heard
yet I sometimes hear it
beneath my skin

IN YOU

Above you
sun moon stars
Beyond them
endless worlds
Beyond the heavens
endless heaven

Above you
what your eyes see
In you
all that is
visible and the
endless invisible

LOVE III

When shall come together again
in the lake
you as water
I as lotus flower

You will carry me
I will drink you

We shall belong together
in the eyes of the world

And even the stars
will stare in wonder
that there are two
who have changed back
into the dream
which chose them

LOVE

Awakened
as voices caught us

fishes flew through our hair
delicately coloured fins
almost flowers

Water bubbled up
from a buried spring
we collected it
in cupped hands
drank of it
the rest ran
through our fingers

drank new courage
refreshed
in pursuit of the voices

above us
still they spoke
strong as stars
frightening

We lay down
with the fishes
took off
all our words

THE ISLAND

As we met
on the island
there were two suns woven
into one tapestry
with the breath of
the water intertwined

In the days of dust
these two suns moved
apart
the island was washed ashore
like a goldfish you lay
in your glass vessel

Then these days faded too
Now I knit the island shore
back into my book

SIX

OLD GREY-HAIRED WOMAN

In the room filled with nothing and no-one
she sits by the window hour after hour

Beyond the pane
is a world of contexts:
houses trees cars people
structures appear
shift
twining and joining
separating then forming again
in the vast context
beyond the pane

The pane lives out its world aloud
they kick it in
step right through it
but still it lives out in defiant sounds
the world of whistles and voices

Shut out from the outside world
the grey-haired woman steps
back into the room
filled with nothing and no-one
Alone in her small room
of wood and whitewash
beneath the frail sun of her lamp
she completes her tiny tasks:
the work of a housewife

Grey as the walls
her fears
are stitched to her mind
the hem grey
in the closed space of her ear
The walls weep the grey
of repetition
bed table chairs
are strangers who have become hostile

Her harshest enemy the mirror
is icily ready
in this roomless room
to take her in
to hold her in the spell
of her frightened eyes
It conceals not a single grey hair
or wrinkle
She looks into her fate of glass
amazed that it does not shatter

COFFINS

Accustomed
to carrying coffins
on my shoulders
heavy
with the waste of these times

I rest now
wooden
in the grass
which carries me
as if I were
a coffin

SIGNS

My skin
tattooed
with jumbled signs

At night
I live in an urn
in which lie
the ashes of the world

Every morning I open
my eyes to the sun

Which arises
and yokes me
to the cogs
of the clock

WHEN I HAVE GONE

When I have gone
the sun might burn still

The planets still move
to their own laws
round a centre
no-one knows

The lilac still smell
as sweet
the snow send out its white rays

When I go away
from our forgetful earth
will you speak my words
a while for me?

EXCHANGE

Who has not known
the stars as calm as this
when night
gives up its dreams
to our sleep

Shadows
fishes
sway in the stream
the flow of sensations

The shapes
of love
and of fear
separate

when night
gives up its sleep
to our dreams

NIGHT

Now the tulip
has closed its door

And Orion's silver apples
have ripened

Now with crystal sounds
the fountain
recreates its shape
of dreams and drops

SEVEN

STILL THE NIGHT

Who says I am singing
I am saying not singing
how lovely in its glass this carnation
as it breathes
the legend on its way

Snow now black
below the pane
still the night has many voices
walls beyond walls

Upon this page
the shadow
is my hand
writing the night
is mere shadow and my partner insists
I should pack
my time is going on a journey

QUESTIONS

I come with
thorny questions
bloodless sun
with thistles and wind

with the queen-ant
and her indignant army
with questions whither and whence

with the hill beneath the stone
with the flickering candle
lips of wax
questions formed of smoke

with strangled love
with the unglazed vessel
stolen from your eyes
the screech of vultures above

I come
to whomever
with questions
why and wherefore

ON THE BARRICADES

We on the barricades
endlessly
the globe turns and turns
joining our revolt
against itself

We patriarchs matriarchs
great-grandchildren
turn the future
on the barricades
of stones
of words
of blood